Help! I've Fallen and Can't Get Up: The Problem

Written by

Julian Richard McCroy Sr.

Table of Contents

Foreword _____ 3
Help! I've Fallen and Can't Get Up: The Problem _ 6
Don't Stay Away Too Long _____ 21
Removing Your Candlestick _____ 27
The Prodigal Son _____ 35
Grab a Hold of GOD'S Hand: the Solution _____ 45
Questions or Thoughts _____ 51
Scriptural Readings: _____ 55

FOREWORD

Psalms 37:23, 24
The steps of a good man are ordered by the LORD: and he delighteth in his way. Though he fall, he shall not be utterly cast down: for the LORD upholdeth him with his hand. KJV

As I sit here and write these words or this book, as I hope to call it. I am convinced that without a shadow of doubt herein lies my blessing to further the understanding of God's word and make my way prosperous. The LORD GOD had directed me some years ago after receiving His Holy Spirit, to instruct the saints and sinners alike on God's word. I failed to do that command and it has cost me greatly (family, divorce, indebtedness, and unlearned people). I have been instructed again to start a writing ministry that the LORD GOD has blessed that will speak to many. First I want everyone to know that "what ever I have received, I have received it from heaven above, so likewise I will not boast as to say this is my knowledge but clearly by revelation of the Holy Spirit will I write to bring glory to GOD, Our Father, and the LORD Jesus Christ, our Savior [1](1 Cor 4:7). Even when we prophecy we do it partially, because that which is perfect (Jesus Christ) has not come again [2](1 Cor 13:9, 10). So I through faith do attempt to somehow explain or expostulate on God's vast Word, as if man can do that. For His ways are past finding out and HIS judgments unsearchable [3](Romans 11:33). I dedicate this book to the obedience that lies in the righteousness of CHRIST who has reconciled us and made us right with GOD, the Father. Just to share something with you I surely know that through affliction you will turn back to the Savior. Please I pray that you approach this book with an open spirit-filled mind and through prayer. I am not

---

[1] See Scripture References
[2] See Scripture References
[3] See Scripture References

a scholar and not a theologian, neither have I attended seminary school. I have sat at the foot of the Master and learned from Him, who teaches and brings to remembrance all things that Christ has said [4](John 14:26) and taught.

Scripture References:

1 Corinthians 4:7
For who maketh thee to differ from another? and what hast thou that thou didst not receive? now if thou didst receive it, why dost thou glory, as if thou hadst not received it?

1 Corinthians 13:9, 10
For we know in part, and we prophesy in part. But when that which is perfect is come, then that which is in part shall be done away.

Romans 11:33
O the depth of the riches both of the wisdom and knowledge of God! how unsearchable are his judgments, and his ways past finding out!

John 14:26
But the Comforter, which is the Holy Ghost, whom the Father will send in my name, he shall teach you all things, and bring all things to your remembrance, whatsoever I have said unto you.

Help! I've Fallen and Can't Get Up: The Problem

---

[4] See Scripture References

(Psalms 13)

Psalms 13:1-6
1)How long wilt thou forget me, O LORD? for ever? how long wilt thou hide thy face from me? 2)How long shall I take counsel in my soul, having sorrow in my heart daily? how long shall mine enemy be exalted over me? 3)Consider and hear me, O LORD my God: lighten mine eyes, lest I sleep the sleep of death; 4)Lest mine enemy say, I have prevailed against him; and those that trouble me rejoice when I am moved. 5)But I have trusted in thy mercy; my heart shall rejoice in thy salvation. 6)I will sing unto the LORD, because he hath dealt bountifully with me. KJV (Authorized)

I received the Spirit of God in 1998 through the laying on of hands by my oldest sister. My life had been changed from sinner to a saint saved by grace. I had my immediate family (wife and children), you know I was on cloud nine when I got saved and confessed Jesus as Lord and Savior of my life. But one thing I didn't realize was that the bible says that after Jesus was baptized with the Holy Spirit He was led immediately into the wilderness to be tempted by the devil [5](Matthew 4). Sometimes we as Christians forget that we will be tested and tried to bring us to perfection. If you truly serve God you will suffer persecution. But glory hallelujah! You will also reign with Him and partake of His inheritance and spiritual blessings [6](Romans 8:17). No one told me that I would be divorced, that my family and friends would call me weird, and that I would experience persecution immediately. I had been called to preach and to evangelism and began to discuss these things with my wife. (Don't discuss what God has told you to do with anyone that is not spiritually minded). For carnal-minded people think carnal-minded. The enemy watches to see where he can attack you and create the most damage. That's why the Word tells us to watch and pray! My life as I had known it began to change for the better, but for me it seemed

---

[5] See Scripture References
[6] See Scripture References

worse. My home began to crumble, I mean the very walls. My wife at the time would not support me in the ministry. She told me I was boring and that all I wanted to do was stay in church and read the bible. I thought that was what she prayed for. I didn't understand at the time that I needed balance, but she needed to be instructed as well. So she told me that she couldn't be a pastor's wife and that I had to choose between her and God. If I chose God she would leave, if I chose her, things would be fine. When the words came out of her mouth I immediately began to pray for her protection for the foolish thing she had said. It is better to serve God alone than with a thousand nay saying church folk. Notice I did not say baptized filled with the Holy Spirit, I said the in the way folk. I prayed for my marriage even after she filed for divorce. She started bringing up old hurtful things of our life together i.e. my infidelity and running the streets. She began also taking up conversation with an old acquaintance. The devil really knows how to pour it on. Where I messed up at wasn't me praying for restoration, but me taking my eye off of God and putting it on man. I would go and talk to pastors and other people who encouraged me to stand strong and not give up on my marriage. It is important that we as spiritual fathers and mothers be equipped with the Word and have the capacity to protect the one that is newborn and weak in faith from the enemy and his wiles. They meant well, but I must say the Lord God will not withhold any good thing from those that walk upright in heart (Psalms 84:11). My wife wasn't trying to reconcile like the Word says. It just wasn't in her and neither was she my wife. We eventually divorced. I began to ask God, "why?" while holding on to my relationship with her, refusing to move on. Not knowing that God had already said, "no!" I began to doubt the Word of God and its sincerity, because of my lack of understanding. I didn't care what this woman did when I was in the world, but when God intervenes in your life, you stand up and become a real man. I had always taken care of her and my children, they wanted for nothing, but I can say I never really loved as she needed to be loved. I didn't realize I didn't love myself until I had the knowledge of God in my life. How can you love someone else if you don't love God or yourself? You can't! at the point of separation, I took my eyes off God and began to just carry on as though He would bring it all back together. I would talk to old acquaintances but I refused to lie with or commit myself to them. My life began to spiral out of control in the area of love and marriage. Because I took my eyes off of the

LORD! Brothers and sisters you have to look to the hills from which cometh your help. I thought when you got saved you would be exempt from what we call bad things happening. But they come more often when you choose to live right. I felt helpless at that time and wanted to know if I should hold on to the hope of reconciliation with my wife. I prayed and prayed for several years about my marriage. I laid with her over a two year period thinking that she would come back. I was a good father to my children and treated her like she was still my wife. My father told me one day, "if you want to get over her and move on with your service to God, stop treating her like she's your wife and stop sleeping with her. She doesn't want you, just wants to control you." Satan really knew how to hurt me at that time. I felt like I had fallen and couldn't get up. Why at a time when I no longer lived like a thug? It seemed as though people liked me better as a presumptuous sinner. I called out, "Help! Help! I've fallen and I can't get up."

> ***Fallen*** – means to be descended, decreased, reduced, collapsed, or lost your footing.

I'm here to tell you that the Lord will answer your prayers for you if you continue to do His will. I was ordained as an itinerant (local) pastor for the A.M.E. denomination, led Men's Bible study, a young people's bible study and outreach. I was just ready to give it all up, wandering how God could take my wife and children from me whom I loved very much. I used to tell people it must be because of past sins. I believe that God forgives sin but there must be an account given on what we do. I believed God took my wife and family and gave it to another man. The only problem was that this man wasn't holy and didn't know Jesus. "Something's wrong! Come on

God can't you see I love her," I said to the Lord. Have you ever been asleep and had a dream that you were falling and couldn't stop? That's exactly how my natural life felt. I finally encouraged myself by preaching to myself and continuing to preach at different locations around the Southern Illinois area. I would hand checks over to her without thinking of myself. I just couldn't get up. So as I was being attacked my faith was being weakened. I was going to pastors and leaders and asking them for counsel to no avail. This dampened my faith. I thought, Lord how can we hear and receive faith to get up and going when our leaders don't know your Word well enough to give counsel to those who sit under them.

After my acceptance of Christ, my family also started acting strange towards me. I would pull up with my children and immediately because of the anointing on my life; they would feel convicted about drinking and smoking weed in front of me. I didn't go to visit to preach to them. I would go to enjoy myself and have relief from this miserable fallen state I had gotten into. They would tell me I was ruining their high and mood. They would mock me by saying, "Here comes the preacher, you all better watch out!" It made me feel alienated from my family. You might lose friends and family when you accept God, believe that! Darkness can't dwell with light! I lost some of my best friends because of my departure from the world of sin. It was very lonely at that time. As you can see, I never gave the solution a chance it was all about me. When we take our eyes off of God then we enter into temptation and fall back into the old man. I tried to run from this hurt by moving to Atlanta, Georgia. I thought, I'll move down here and God will show me my ministry and my wife. So I joined a church without God's advice. Women tried to date me and I went on dates with some. So I tried hanging out with the world and begin to party a little bit. (You shouldn't party while you are in training with the LORD!) I began to take on some of the things that I had asked God to deliver me from, just to be accepted. I read my bible less, hopped from church to church, and began to drink. I began to indulge in pornography and indulge in self-pleasure from time to time. I had really had begun to compromise my faith and take my walk with Christ nonchalantly. When you grieve the Spirit of God and walk in disobedience after hearing His voice God will stop talking. If you're not careful you can have your conscience seared and be given over to a reprobate mind. The enemy of our soul wants us to be miserable and unforgiven like he is. We really have to be careful and return to the Lord quickly. I was mad at the Lord because of the things I thought He let go on in my life. I didn't realize it was my fault for letting the enemy in and not keeping my eyes on God. I began to be disgruntled and not want any friends, let alone a woman. I didn't even want to be a father to my children. I felt that God would only tease me with them and take them from me also. I stopped talking to Christian people and praying. I had given up because I couldn't see me getting up. While I was in Atlanta my children after staying a brief period with me moved with their mother to Savannah, Georgia. My children were not taken to church, not required to study the bible, and were allowed to be around unsaved and ungodly influences. I felt like someone had dropped a ton of weights on my chest. I really thought that there was no use to pray. I had gotten so far from God, that He would hear me anyway. It was because of my sin (past and present) that Satan, was having a field day with my children. I thought, Lord, have I really done that much that you would allow Satan to destroy my children. I had fallen and couldn't get up. I looked at the problem and not the solution, because I had stopped serving God with all my might and just went through the motions. I became even more bitter and said why should I be thankful to God, it would be better off to be dead instead of continuing to go through this. That's just what the devil wants you to do, but the devil is a liar! God has the last say in all of our affairs, whether you're saved or not. Remember the Word says that God is able to keep that which you have committed to Him. It also says that we are sealed with the Holy Spirit unto the day of redemption. So even in my despondency I had to still look up and try to reach for God's hand. The Spirit of God would tell me that He loved me and that I was still his and that I still would be used. I just didn't believe it, I had learned to lie on my back too much and didn't have the strength to reach up (pray and fasting) and grab God's hand.

Scripture References:

Matthew 4:
Then was Jesus led up of the Spirit into the wilderness to be tempted of the devil.

Romans 8:17
And if children, then heirs; heirs of God, and joint-heirs with Christ; if so be that we suffer with him, that we may be also glorified together.

Notes

Notes

Don't Stay Away Too Long
(The Book of Judges)
Judges 2:7-13

7)And the people served the LORD all the days of Joshua, and all the days of the elders that outlived Joshua, who had seen all the great works of the LORD, that he did for Israel. 8)And Joshua the son of Nun, the servant of the LORD, died, being an hundred and ten years old. 9)And they buried him in the border of his inheritance in Timnathheres, in the mount of Ephraim, on the north side of the hill Gaash. 10)And also all that generation were gathered unto their fathers: and there arose another generation after them, which knew not the LORD, nor yet the works which he had done for Israel. 11)And the children of Israel did evil in the sight of the LORD, and served Baalim: 12)And they forsook the LORD God of their fathers, which brought them out of the land of Egypt, and followed other gods, of the gods of the people that were round about them, and bowed themselves unto them, and provoked the LORD to anger. 13)And they forsook the LORD, and served Baal and Ashtaroth.

We as human beings have a knack for being creatures of habit. This is proven in our methods of learning, training, etc. If you have fallen away from God, it is of the utmost importance to return to Him quickly. When we are not in God's presence we suffer greatly. The blessings that He has for you at the appointed time are passed over by you, because you are spiritually blind and deaf. You stayed away too long from the Source that is vital for your very existence. Your mind has become cloudy; you're lethargic, and empty. You've stayed away too long! God is always speaking to us in different ways but when we are carnal minded we can't understand spiritual things. It's a sad thing to be without discernment. You're just another Balaam that has forgotten the sole purpose of being a prophet. He stayed away from God too long enjoying the meager passing perks to curse Israel (Apple of God's Eye). Israel and its sister Judah played the harlot with other nations. They began to run after the wrong thing instead of the One Thing. Even after being advised by numerous prophets of the impending results. But in the frailty of life and its temporary pleasures we fall away from God. Israel and Judah were in a state of apostasy, where they killed and mocked the messengers of God. The reason being they had been away too long! When we stay away too long we begin to do what we think is right in our own eyes. So there is a period in our lives like Israel where there is no judgment given. Solomon, the wisest human being beside the Lord Jesus who has ever lived on earth began to walk after the gods of the women he became involved with. Solomon confessed because he stayed away too long from God's wisdom, that all is vanity outside of God's presence. We need to get the picture of staying away from God. It would be like taking the oxygen out of the air, you wouldn't be able to breathe. It would be like eating food with no nourishment or filling, you would forever be eating and malnourished. When we plan our way to always hear from God our way will be prosperous. If you have a lamp in a dark room where there are no windows for the light to shine in and you choose not to plug into the source (God) that can turn on the lamp you're without vision. When we stay away too long after falling away we are like the foolish person that will sit in that dark room when the Light you need is already there in your presence. Turn the light on my friend, God hasn't left you, but you have left Him. Don't stay away too long!

Notes

Notes

Removing Your Candlestick
(Revelation 2: 4, 5)

Revelation 2:4, 5

4)Nevertheless I have somewhat against thee, because thou hast left thy first love. 5)Remember therefore from whence thou art fallen, and repent, and do the first works; or else I will come unto thee quickly, and will remove thy candlestick out of his place, except thou repent.

My Son come out of the way of the world for My calling for you is great. Turn back unto me quickly or I'll remove your candlestick out of its place because you have left your first love. Even though you have the iniquity and evildoers of Satan to blame, you left Me (Jesus Christ). This is the word I heard clearly in my spirit from the Lord.

God is calling us to higher calling in our walk with Him! The choice is yours, either you love Him or you don't. The bible says, "Choose you this day whom you will serve the Lord God or the world." The bible tells us that the Lord is here and waiting for us to be with Him and for Him. However if we don't return to Him quickly from our fallen state, we could and will have our candlestick removed out of its place. The Lord Jesus in the book of Revelation was telling John that those of us that have once believed in Him and trusted in His name have left Him, our First love. Unless we return to Him quickly He will remove our candlestick out of its place. A candlestick, your candlestick is what burns in front of the Lord's presence, however if its wick is dry and the light is growing dim it is of no use to the Lord.

> *Candlestick* – means your lampstand that reflects you in the presence of the Lord JESUS!

The reason is because you are offensive to Him at this state; you're causing the other candlesticks to have to accommodate your inability to cast off light. The Lord is the light of the world and that light is the life of man. God has already begun to prune the vines and cut off all that are not producing fruit. So we must produce fruit that is suitable and give light from that oil that is given from the Holy Spirit to do His work for the kingdom of Heaven. When we are in a fallen unrepentant state we are not burning the lamp continually before the Lord. The Lord gave the command to the Levites to always have the lamps burning in the Tabernacle of meeting in front of the Holy of Holies [7](Lev 24:2). You are a priest or priestess in the kingdom of God; you must keep the lamp or candlestick burning. When there is no oil being poured in by the Holy Spirit your candlestick or lamp will not give off a soothing savor or aroma. When your life is filled with sin it has a stench to it that is offensive to the LORD. Nothing that offends

---

[7] See Scripture References

can dwell with the Lord or in His presence. Keep the oil of joy and obedience flowing into the lamp stand, so that it can keep burning hot. When the Lord removes the candlestick out of its place, the oil eventually dries up and the pleasant aroma evaporates. You are then in a state of "Ichabod" meaning the Spirit of God has departed from you [8](1 Sam 4:21).

> ***Ichabod*** – means the glory of the Lord God is departed gone. No power left for this place.

This is blasphemy against the Holy Spirit, in which you can't be forgiven of in this world or the world to come. The reason being is you have tasted of the blessings of heaven; you have witnessed the power of the Holy Spirit and its comfort. Now to just turn away from it and neglect it because of your

---

[8] See Scripture References

fallen state is a slap in the face of God. You haven't anything to look forward to but a fiery indignation and wrath for there remains no more sacrifice [9](Heb 10:26). Your conscience becomes seared with a hot iron, and you no longer retain God in any of your thoughts. This is the mind state of being reprobate. Although you may live on some years, nothing you do will prosper, and you will just wander; all because you had your candlestick removed out of its place!! This leads me to tell you to look from afar off and see the Kingdom of God and all of its blessings and come home, Prodigal Son or Daughter, come home!

Scripture References:

Leviticus 24:1, 2:
1) And the LORD spake unto Moses, saying, 2) Command the children of Israel, that they bring unto

---

[9] See Scripture References

thee pure oil olive beaten for the light, to cause the lamps to burn continually.

1 Samuel 4:21:
And she named the child Ichabod, saying, The glory is departed from Israel: because the ark of God was taken, and because of her father in law and her husband

Hebrews 10:26,27:
26) For if we sin wilfully after that we have received the knowledge of the truth, there remaineth no more sacrifice for sins, 27) But a certain fearful looking for of judgment and fiery indignation, which shall devour the adversaries.

Notes

Notes

The Prodigal Son
(Luke 15)

Luke 15:11-16
11) And he said, A certain man had two sons: 12) And the younger of them said to his father, Father, give me the portion of goods that falleth to me. And he divided unto them his living 13) And not many days after the younger son gathered all together, and took his journey into a far country, and there wasted his substance with riotous living. 14) And when he had spent all, there arose a mighty famine in that land; and he began to be in want. 15) And he went and joined himself to a citizen of that country; and he sent him into his fields to feed swine. 16) And he would fain have filled his belly with the husks that the swine did eat: and no man gave unto him.

Prodigal – means to be excommunicated or to forsake take leave, depart.

To be prodigal (fallen away) is to enjoy the pleasures of sin for a season, believe me they don't last forever. The blessings and talents that God has given us for the kingdom of God, you and I have shared them and blessed the world with them. However, we didn't know that we were cursing ourselves for mixing light with darkness. We take the inheritance or provision that God has for us and go squander it on the temporal observant things on this earth, you know all that we ever wanted. Until the season comes to an end and our money runs out.

That is how we do God when we choose to fall away from Him due to the pleasures of sin, lack of faith, and us sitting on the fence. In our falling state we often like to stay in the prodigal sense. We seem to think that we know what is best for us and not God. I thought, hey! I'll kick it a little and then I'll go back to God. At that time, the God thing is not so popular, plus I'd tried it and it seemed that the way of God would let you down. I was divorced; my children had been hurt. My mother passed away and I didn't have any friends. In instances like these, we think why not just live riotous, after all nobody has ever cared for us especially God. If God cared so much, then why is all this happening to us? All the while in our blind state not realizing that the Lord misses us and is looking for His lost sheep. He is sweeping the house but still no coin and He has gone onto the high cliffs still no sheep. The Lord has even gone into the predator's (satan) territory to see perhaps if we have been torn. We have hid the eyes of God from us because of our sin [10](Isaiah 59). He wants to grab us and hold us but He won't hold us against our will. He (JESUS) prays for the Father to keep us and makes intercession for us. Our money runs out and we find the world is not so pleasant and thrilling and that very thing we trusted in has just pricked our hand. The one we counted on has given up the ghost. Now the very ones that we shared your fortune with have gotten all they want out of us and can't use us anymore. They kick us out and don't feed us. We have no place to stay or

---

[10] See Scripture Reference

food to eat. We hire ourselves out to the enemy to survive still not ready to go back home and say sorry. You see we have fallen and can't get up. It wouldn't be right to admit that our Father knows what's best for us. If we admit that we are wrong then that would be calling ourselves a liar and God be truth. No, we just keep working for meager wages and eating pig slop. We can't wash our hands or faces and there is no fatted calf for us. Our once princely robe fit for royalty has become tainted and eventually is sold to the boss. We have forgotten how blessed we were in our Father's house; we have grown accustomed to what the world offers. Then one day we have even been denied the pig's slop and we begin to walk after getting up because of our hunger. Hunger will make us do a lot of things we didn't think we would. We walk until we see a pond of fresh water, at this time we refresh our eyes, quench our thirst, then after washing our face we can see a clearer. We see smoke rising with the aroma of fresh food cooking. Along there is the tall structures soundly built and fortified. These structures magnificent in glory and wisdom stand very tall. We began to think after the water has washed the crust and dirt from our eyes and can see afar. We say to ourselves, "this is my Father's house. I must go home because I'm living real foul. I need to get up and dust myself off. I will make amends with my Father and confess that I've sinned against Him and Him alone." Perhaps our Father will forgive us and welcome us back in. After all we still have rotten corn in our teeth and I smell torrid.

We began to walk towards our Father's house. While we are struggling to get up from the fallen stat, the boss (enemy) shows a prostitute's bare leg, he promises better food and wages, even tells us that we can stay there in his palace until we get our own. Nevertheless the chattering and cheering we hear from our Father's house is a like a fire or light to us as moths. We run quickly towards this place trying to get the smell out of our nose and vomit the undigested food in our stomachs to make room for the feast that the Father has already begin to prepare. He has swept the house again and found the lost coins. He has found on top of a ragged cliff some scared sheep that are malnourished because the grass is not any good up there. Now in His rejoicing He has sounded the alarm, called His friends and family, killed the fatted calf, and prepared the ring and robe for us. We need to understand that God has and is waiting for us to get up and come home. So we can fall on His neck and cry to Him saying, "Sorry Father, I have sinned against You and You alone foolishly and lost all that I am and have."

Please, we ask to be received back into His home and presence. He readily agrees for God loves us unconditionally, and even will quiet His other children that have been there when they began to complain about us and our waywardness. We have to be like the Prodigal and get home to God! God has helped and we can get up and make it; God is holding His hand out for us. You see in this state of fallen we are dead. But God has received (found) us to Himself as alive again.

The answer is to run quickly home son or daughter to the One who cares for us continually. Then we will be able to get up from this state and grab hold of His unchanging all powerful hand. Get Up! Get Up! Get Up! The Hand is there!!! Hallelujah!!! Glory be to the Most High God who is blessed forever.

Scripture References:

Isaiah 59:1, 2:

1) Behold, the LORD'S hand is not shortened, that it cannot save; neither his ear heavy, that it cannot hear: 2) But your iniquities have separated between you and your God, and your sins have hid his face from you, that he will not hear.

Notes

Notes

Grab a Hold of GOD'S Hand: the Solution

Now that we have come to ourselves or senses we can and have gotten up. I have to say even after all that we do, there is nothing that can separate us from the love of the LORD GOD! [11](Romans 8:38). I know this may sound strange but God is ready and willing to forgive our sins. It was that desire that was hidden deep within me that I had clouded by sin and getting off of the track that had to come forth. God has a plan for all of us a good plan to prosper us [12](Jeremiah 29:11). So the Lord through these afflictions let me see how far I had fallen into the miry pit and could not get up without His help. This is an act of faith in the Word of God. For He says I'll never leave you nor forsake you! [13](Hebrews 13:5). You can take a hold of God's unchanging

---

[11] See Scripture References
[12] See Scripture References
[13] See Scripture References

hand and get out of the miry pit. For we know that the steps of a good man are ordered by God, and He delights in his way and though he fall the Lord won't utterly cast him down, for the Lord will hold him in His hand [14](Psalms 37:23,24). Our Father doesn't do anything in vain He wouldn't save you for nothing! You and I have to literally trust the Lord GOD in every situation. For there is no other salvation under the heavens or in the earth but Jesus Christ! He is the only one that can bring us back to that obedience that was once in us. We have to stay focused on the love and work of God in our life. When we are so busy doing the work of the Lord we are too tired and busy to worry about what's going on in our lives. We have learned from our fallen state that if we take our eyes off of the Lord we will begin to sink as Peter did when he asked

---

[14] See Scripture References

Jesus to let him walk to Him on water. Peter after he grabbed a hold of the Lord's hand, he was able to stand on the water. For it is the Lord who is able to still the waters and make it be like concrete. Jesus created all things in the earth including you, so why not let Him figure it out and us just trust Him. He promises to never leave us or forsake us, and be with us even to the ends of the worlds. God is faithful and will not hold any good thing from us that walk upright in heart. I adjure you all to grab the hand that reaches for you when you fall. You can **get up** because He promises to not utterly cast us down but to hold us up in His hand. No one or nothing can take you out of the Father's hand [15](John 10: 28, 29); you're safe in His hands. God is merciful and waiting to welcome you home again.

---

[15] See Scripture References

Scripture References:

Romans 8:38:
For I am persuaded, that neither death, nor life, nor angels, nor principalities, nor powers, nor things present, nor things to come,

Jeremiah 29:11:
For I know the thoughts that I think toward you, saith the LORD, thoughts of peace, and not of evil, to give you an expected end.

Hebrews 13:5:
Let your conversation be without covetousness; and be content with such things as ye have: for He hath said, I will never leave thee, nor forsake thee.

Psalms 37:23, 24:
23) The steps of a good man are ordered by the LORD: and he delighteth in his way. 24) Though he fall, he shall not be utterly cast down: for the LORD upholdeth him with his hand.

John 10:28, 29:
And I give unto them eternal life; and they shall never perish, neither shall any man pluck them out of my hand. 29) My Father, which gave them me, is greater than all; and no man is able to pluck them out of my Father's hand.

Notes

Notes

Questions or Thoughts

1. How has your life in the past or present made you feel like you have fallen and can't get up at all? Do you feel like God has forsaken you? Do you think that God has forgotten you?

_____
_____
_____
_____
_____
_____
_____
_____
_____

2. How do you plan to deal with the situation at hand when you feel like this?

_____
_____
_____

4. Do you understand that when you answer the calling of God in your life many friends and family alike will began to find you not so popular?

_____
_____
_____

5. Will you believe what the Lord God says or what your flesh or what the enemy is telling you in your time of distress?

_____
_____
_____

_____

6. Do you understand that there are many other Christians that feel as we do in certain stressful times?

_____
_____
_____

_____

7. The author of Hebrews tells us of the danger of falling away from God after tasting the goodness of the Holy Spirit. This should rest heavily on the Christian mind, because God is not mocked. How do you plan to keep your mind on serving God even when it feels like you are without God's help.

_____
_____
_____

_____

8. Do you feel victorious now having studied the scriptures and reading this book?

_____
_____
_____

_____

9. Have you ever gone to someone in the church that you assumed that was full of all knowledge and counsel and they couldn't give you any word?

_____
_____
_____
_____

10. How does studying to show yourself approved affect those that are coming behind you?

_____
_____
_____
_____

11. Has the enemy ever tried to tempt you to leave the church because of another person's sin or falling? How did this affect your walk?

_____
_____
_____
_____

12. Have you ever tried to hold on to someone or something that you have clearly heard and understood that the LORD GOD is saying, "NO"?

_____
_____

13. In what ways has the enemy tried to attack your faith outside of you (family, friends, etc)?

_____
_____
_____
_____

14. Have you ever witnessed anyone taking pleasure in your present troubles? (Remember misery loves company)

_____
_____
_____
_____

Scriptural Readings:

1 Corinthians 4:7
Isaiah 59
1 Corinthians 13: 9, 10
Romans 8:38
Romans 11:33
Jeremiah 29:11
John 14:26
Hebrews 13:5
Matthew 4
Psalms 37:23, 24
Psalms 13
Psalms 84:11
Romans 8:17
The Book of Judges
Revelation 2: 4, 5
Lev 24:2
1 Sam 4:21
Heb 26:10
Luke 15

www.ingramcontent.com/pod-product-compliance
Lightning Source LLC
Chambersburg PA
CBHW072037060426
42449CB00010BA/2310